P9-DEQ-012

READING STREET
Sleuth
COMMON CORE

PEARSON

Glenview, Illinois
Boston, Massachusetts
Chandler, Arizona
Upper Saddle River, New Jersey

Acknowledgments appear on page 78, which constitutes an extension of this copyright page.

ISBN-13: 978-0-328-73055-1
ISBN-10:   0-328-73055-6
2 3 4 5 6 7 8 9 10 V003 16 15 14 13 12

Contents

From: The Super Sleuths
Subject: Mysteries

Dear Junior Sleuthhound,

Mysteries are all around. There could be a mystery on your playground. There could be a mystery in a faraway land. There could be mysteries between the pages of this book! So what do you do to solve a mystery? Become a sleuthhound! Look for clues. Ask interesting questions. Then put all the pieces together and prove your answers. This book gives you a chance to practice skills that sleuths use. As you read this book use the Super Sleuth Steps to find answers to some really big questions!

Good luck!

SUPER SLEUTH STEPS

Look for Clues

- Look back through the text and pictures. What do they tell you?

- Write or draw what you learn. It will help you remember.

- Look for important ideas and try to put the clues together.

Ask Questions

- Super sleuths ask great questions.

- Be curious.

- Try to find out more.

Make Your Case

- Look at all the clues and summarize what you know.

- Use what you learn and already know to think of your own ideas.

- Tell what you think.

Prove It!

- Show what you have learned.

- Work with others. Share the adventure!

Unit 1
Exploration

Hi, Sleuthhounds!
In this unit, you will be looking for clues as we explore new places and things. Here are some sleuth tips to help you. Enjoy the adventure!

Sleuth Tips

Look for Clues

Where do sleuths find clues?

- Sleuths look at the words. Some clues may be hidden.
- Sleuths find clues in the pictures. Look closely.

Ask Questions

What kinds of questions do sleuths ask?

- Sleuths ask what happened.
- Sleuths try to learn when, where, why, and how something happened.

Make Your Case

How do sleuths decide on an answer?

- Sleuths look back at what they read. They think about what they already know.
- Sleuths look at the clues. Clues may point to the best answer.

Prove It!

What do sleuths do to prove what they know?

- Sleuths think about all they have learned and decide what is important to share.
- Sleuths plan what they will share and check their work.

The Pilsen area in Chicago has a rich history. Over the years, people from many parts of the world have come here. Then, in the 1950s, more and more people from Mexico began moving here. They came to find work and to help their families. Newcomers brought their music and food. They brought their traditions. But they did something more. They made Pilsen a work of art.

Now Pilsen is a very large Mexican American community. Almost every street in Pilsen has a colorful mural. A mural is a large painting on a wall. You can see these paintings on schools and churches. You can find them on bridges and in parks. They even cover apartment buildings and houses. They are everywhere you look!

8

Many Pilsen murals show ideas that are important to the people here. You can learn about Mexican history and heroes. You can see how important it is to work hard and help others. One bright mural shows a family cooking a meal. Another shows people working at their jobs. Some murals show old Mexican stories. The murals show that Mexican American culture is alive and well in Pilsen!

Be a Sleuth

Look for Clues Why did the author write this selection? Use clues from the text in your answer.

Ask Questions What interesting questions would you ask the artists of the murals in Pilsen?

Make Your Case What is the most important lesson or idea murals tell us about a community? Explain your answer using clues from the text.

Down the Space Drain

Have you ever seen water going down a drain? It goes around and around. Finally, it slips down the pipe. Something like this happens in space too. These "space drains" are called black holes.

Black holes aren't really holes. They are places in space where gravity is very strong. Gravity is a force that pulls things toward Earth. It is what makes things fall down instead of floating up when we drop them.

A black hole forms when a giant star gets very old. The star starts to shrink. Its gravity gets stronger and stronger. This super-strong gravity makes the star get so small that it can't be seen. It pulls other things toward the star. It pulls in space dust, gas, and nearby stars. These things circle around and get closer. Gravity pulls them apart. Soon, they seem to disappear into the black hole.

There may even be a black hole in our galaxy. But don't worry. It is very far away from Earth. We won't be going down any space drains anytime soon!

Be a Sleuth

Look for Clues What clues in the text help you understand how strong the pull of gravity is in a black hole?

Ask Questions Talk with a partner. Talk about two interesting questions you have about stars and black holes.

Make Your Case What is the most interesting object in space? Explain your choice. Help others understand why it is interesting.

11

The South Pole Adventure of Bothie the Polar Dog

I am Bothie, the Polar Dog, and I am going to tell you about my adventure in Antarctica with my owners, Ranulph and Ginny Fiennes. They had big plans. They wanted to go all the way around the world, and they wanted me to come along.

We sailed to Antarctica in January 1980. It was a strange frozen land of snow and ice. The wind was very strong. The air was so cold that I could freeze in a minute. The Fiennes got me a special polar suit. It even had thick booties to protect my feet.

Our first job was to set up camp. We had three cardboard huts with special layers to keep the heat inside. The snow helped protect us too. We were very snug in our huts.

The team set up radios and other equipment at camp. I had different jobs to do. I visited the cook for food scraps. I cheered people up. I even met a penguin! I have to admit that I was a little shy.

Ranulph went ahead of us. After two months, he finally reached the South Pole. Ginny and I flew there to join him. I left my paw prints at the South Pole!

Be a Sleuth

Ask Questions You learned about one of Bothie's adventures. What are two questions you have about Bothie's adventures with Ranulph and Ginny?

Look for Clues What clues tell you what Antarctica is like?

Make Your Case Would having a pet on an adventure in Antarctica be good or harmful for the pet? Use at least one clue from the story to explain your answer.

LOLOMI AND THE GIANTS

The Moqui people lived in a beautiful desert. Mean giants came to live on the mesa there. They could see all the land from the top of the mesa. If the people went hunting, the giants threw stones. If they traveled on the roads, the giants tried to catch them. The people couldn't go anywhere safely.

One day a young man named Lolomi was walking alone. He saw a horned toad trapped under a rock. He lifted the rock to help it. To Lolomi's surprise, the horned toad spoke.

"Would you like to get rid of the giants?" he asked.

"Yes," Lolomi said.

The lizard gave Lolomi spikes like those on his own head as a helmet. He gave Lolomi armor that was tough like lizard skin. Then he told Lolomi how to beat the giants.

Lolomi went out to meet the giants. The first one he saw tried to scare Lolomi. The giant threw rocks. The rocks bounced off Lolomi's helmet. The giant threw his spear. It couldn't harm Lolomi because of his armor. The giants were afraid of the brave warrior. They ran away and were never seen again.

Thanks to the horned toad, Lolomi became a hero. The Moqui people could now live in peace.

BE A SLEUTH

Look for Clues What clues show that this story could not have really happened?

Ask Questions What do you know about horned toads and lizards? Think of two interesting questions to ask about horned toads.

Make Your Case What is the most important lesson this story teaches? Explain your answer using clues from the text.

Gregor Mendel

Gregor Mendel always loved nature. He grew up on a farm. He walked through the countryside every day. He loved to look at plants and animals along the way. He noticed the ways plants are alike and different. Later, Mendel became a teacher and scientist.

One day Mendel took a long walk. He saw a flower that was different from others of the same kind. It made him wonder. What caused such differences? He began to grow pea plants as part of an experiment. In seven years, he grew thousands of plants! He kept track of different traits in plants. He noticed the color of the flowers and pea pods. He measured the height of the plants. He noticed the shape of their pods and leaves. He saw that there was a pattern. "Parent" plants passed traits to "daughter" plants in certain ways. Mendel's studies helped him discover rules about how traits are passed on. This was the beginning of a branch of science called genetics.

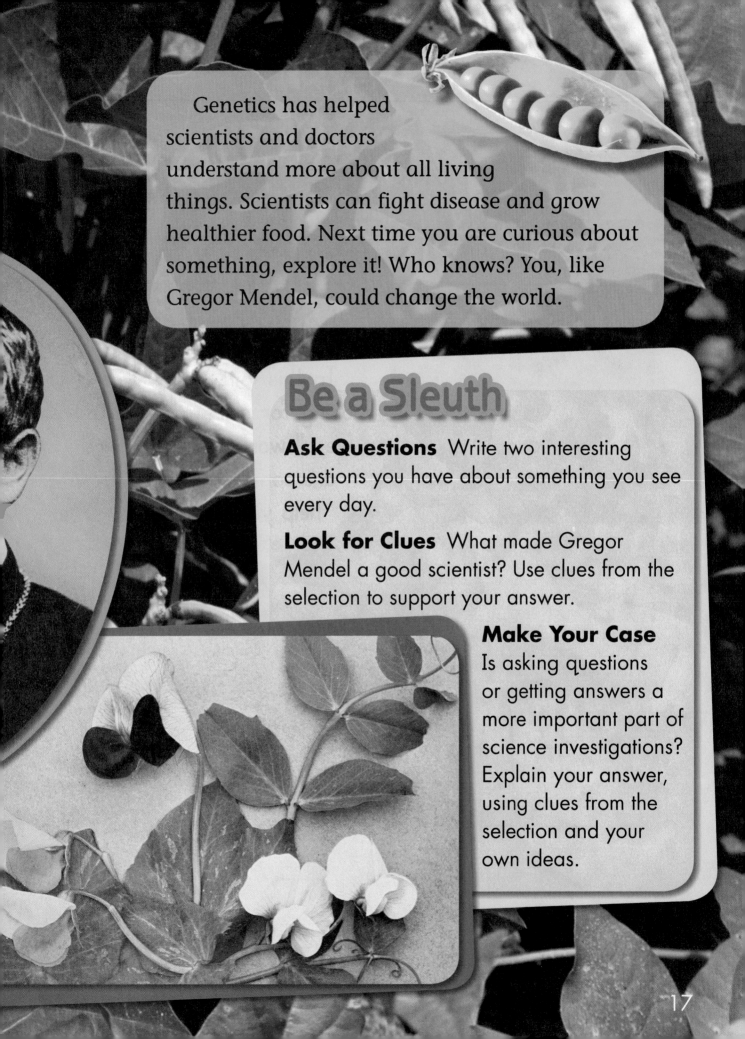

Genetics has helped scientists and doctors understand more about all living things. Scientists can fight disease and grow healthier food. Next time you are curious about something, explore it! Who knows? You, like Gregor Mendel, could change the world.

Be a Sleuth

Ask Questions Write two interesting questions you have about something you see every day.

Look for Clues What made Gregor Mendel a good scientist? Use clues from the selection to support your answer.

Make Your Case Is asking questions or getting answers a more important part of science investigations? Explain your answer, using clues from the selection and your own ideas.

Unit 2
Working Together

Hello, Sleuthhounds!

In this unit, you will be looking for clues to learn how we all work together. Here are some sleuth tips to help you. Good luck!

Sleuth Tips

Look for Clues

Why do sleuths reread?

- Sleuths reread because they know they may miss something the first time.
- Sleuths reread to find hidden clues!

Ask Questions

What makes a great question?

- Sleuths know that a great question is focused on the topic.
- Sleuths choose their words carefully when they ask a question.

Make Your Case

How do sleuths make a clear case?

- Sleuths clearly state what they believe at the beginning and again at the end.
- Sleuths tell the clues they found in the text and pictures.

Prove It!

What do sleuths do when they work with other sleuths?

- Sleuths share what they know. This is the time to share your clues with others.
- Sleuths share the work so everyone gets a chance to shine!

A Real-Life Action Hero

Eric listened closely to the first-aid lesson at his Cub Scout meeting. The guest speaker was talking about the Heimlich maneuver. This action can help someone who is choking. It causes whatever is caught in the choking person's throat to come out. Later Eric saw a television program that taught him more about it. He practiced with his mother. He followed the Cub Scout motto "Be prepared." He had no idea how important that lesson would be.

One day Eric's little sister Jessie was having a snack. Their mother heard Jessie choking. Jessie could not breathe. Nothing their mother did helped.

She called for Eric's help. Then she rushed to call 9-1-1. But Eric was ready. Before his mother could tell the 9-1-1 operator what was happening, Eric sprang into action. He wrapped his arms around Jessie from behind. He did exactly what he had practiced with his mother. The egg Jessie had been eating popped right out! Jessie was safely breathing again. Ten-year-old Eric was a hero.

Be a Sleuth

Look for Clues Why is the order of the events important in this selection? Use clues from the text in your answer.

Ask Questions What are two questions you have about what to do in a home emergency?

Make Your Case Who do you think is a hero? Give reasons why that person is a hero. What qualities does your hero have in common with Eric?

Journey to FREEDOM

In 1854, William was an African American slave in North Carolina. He longed to be free, but that did not seem possible. Late one night, a friend woke up William. He wanted William to escape with him to Canada.

The thought of freedom made William joyful. But how would he and his friend get to Canada? It was hundreds of miles away. They had very little money or food. They had no maps. Where would they hide along the way? Soldiers and other people were looking everywhere for runaway slaves. The answer to his questions was the Underground Railroad.

The Underground Railroad was not a railroad. It was a network of people. The network helped enslaved people escape to freedom. Some "conductors" on the railroad led enslaved people by foot or wagon to safe places. Other people opened their homes and barns to give shelter. Some gave money, clothes, and food to help. Before the end of slavery in the United States, thousands of people used the Underground Railroad to escape slavery.

Even with all that help, the path to freedom was not easy. The trip often took weeks. It was very dangerous. Many of the people who used the railroad agreed that the long journey was a small price to pay for freedom.

Be a Sleuth

Look for Clues What words from the text help you understand how hard it was to escape from slavery?

Ask Questions What is one question you have about the Underground Railroad? Where could you learn more about it?

Make Your Case Escaping from slavery was against the law. Helping enslaved people escape was against the law. Do you think it is ever right to break a law? Explain your thinking.

Making a Difference, ONE BAG at a TIME

When Annie Wignall was eleven, her mother told her something that made her sad. She said that some children have to leave their homes in hard times. They often must leave everything behind. They lose many things that they love and need. Annie wanted to do something to help.

Annie made cute cloth bags for children in need. She found people to donate new items that children might miss from their homes. Annie filled the bags

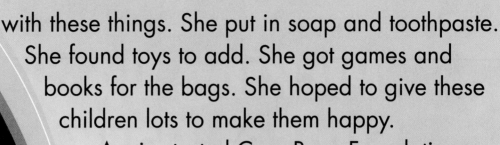

with these things. She put in soap and toothpaste. She found toys to add. She got games and books for the bags. She hoped to give these children lots to make them happy.

Annie started Care Bags Foundation. Every month Annie and other helpers prepare about one hundred Care Bags 4 Kids. Some people sew the bags. Others give things to put in the bags. Volunteers help fill them. The bags are then given to children in need. They bring many smiles!

Care Bags Foundation also helps children in another way. It teaches kids how to make a difference. It tells how to start a Care Bags project in their own towns. Care Bags Foundation has made a big difference with each small bag!

Be a Sleuth

Look for Clues What are two events in the text that caused something else to happen?

Ask Questions What are two questions you would ask Annie Wignall to find out more about the Care Bags Foundation?

Make Your Case Should all children in school be required to participate in a service program during the school year? Explain your reasons.

Picking Up Sunset Park

Lacey stood at the gate of Sunset Park. What she saw made her want to cry. The storm had knocked down two small trees and scattered branches everywhere.

Her brother, Jared, looked at the mess. "We might as well go home," he said. "It's going to be a while before we can play here again."

"Let's pick up some of the branches," Lacey said.

"That will take all day!" Jared said.

"If we work together, we can get it done quickly," Lacey said.

They began to pick up branches and pile them near the gate. As the pile grew, their friends Marius and Elsa rode by.

"What's going on?" Marius asked.

"The storm blew down some trees," Lacey said. "We're cleaning up."

Marius and Elsa hopped off their bikes and began working. Soon, some neighbors saw the kids at work. They started to help clean up too. Mrs. Cleary came with cold lemonade for everyone. Before long, the branches were all cleared. The adults cut the fallen trees and moved them to the side. The park was almost as good as new. Lacey and Jared happily ran to the swings. They were thrilled. There was even time to play before dinner!

Be a Sleuth

Look for Clues What clues in the story tell you how bad the storm damage was?

Ask Questions What are two questions you would ask one of the neighbors who stopped to help?

Make Your Case Whose responsibility was it to clean up the park? Give reasons for your answer.

The Hunt for Amelia's Ring

"Janine, have you seen my ring?" Amelia asked.

Janine *had* seen her sister's ring. She had tried it on, but it was a little big, so she took it off . . . but where did she put it? Janine couldn't remember! When she told her sister the truth, Amelia was upset. Janine had to find that ring! She crawled under tables, peeked inside dresser drawers, looked behind the couch, and opened every cabinet. Finally, she gave up and went outside to sit on the front steps.

Her neighbor, Mrs. Kim, came up the stairs. "What's wrong?" she asked. Janine told her.

"I find it is useful to retrace my steps when I can't find something," Mrs. Kim said.

Janine thought and thought. First, she had done homework, and then she had a snack. Then . . . ah, ha! She remembered!

Janine helped carry Mrs. Kim's groceries. Then she ran to her apartment and went to the kitchen windowsill. There it was! The ring was right where Janine had left it when she helped water Mom's plants. Janine ran to give it to Amelia. She had learned her lesson about taking what wasn't hers. She also learned that two heads are better than one when there is a mystery to solve!

Be a Sleuth

Look for Clues How did Mrs. Kim's suggestion help Janine find the ring? Look for clues in the text.

Ask Questions What are three questions you would ask a person who has lost something?

Make Your Case Which lesson that Janine learned is the most important one? Give reasons to support your answer.

Unit 3
Creative Ideas

Hello there, Sleuthhounds!

In this unit, you will be looking for clues about some creative solutions. Here are some sleuth tips to help you. Have fun!

Sleuth Tips

Look for Clues

How do sleuths get clues from pictures?

- Sleuths use pictures to help them figure out harder words or ideas.
- Sleuths look at pictures to learn things that are not included in the text.

Ask Questions

Why are sleuths so curious?

- Sleuths always wonder why or how something happened. They try to find something others didn't notice.
- Sleuths know that being curious and asking questions can lead to adventures!

Make Your Case

Why don't all sleuths agree on the answers?

- Sleuths may find different clues or put the clues together in different ways.
- Sleuths know that our different experiences cause each of us to think differently.

Prove It!

How can sleuths be creative when showing what they have learned?

- Sleuths try to use new and different ways to show details clearly.
- Sleuths think of many ways to share what they know. They might draw, write, or put on a show!

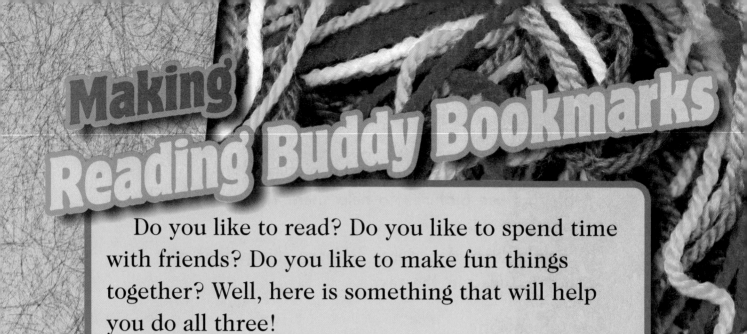

Making Reading Buddy Bookmarks

Do you like to read? Do you like to spend time with friends? Do you like to make fun things together? Well, here is something that will help you do all three!

You will need the help of an adult and the following materials:

- a large paper clip for each of you
- yarn
- scissors
- a ruler
- craft glue
- googly eyes

1. First, cut the yarn into lengths of 8 inches each. If you have thick yarn, you may only need three or four pieces. If you have thin yarn, you may need as many as 20.

2. Then, hold all but one of the strands together. Pull them through the top of the paper clip. (This is the end with only one bend.)

3. Next, bunch the strands together, and tie them with the last piece of yarn. Make the knot very close to the paper clip.

4. Then, glue the googly eyes to the yarn.

5. Last, tie or decorate the yarn any way you like.

Now you have a reading buddy bookmark. Put it to use! Mark your place in a book you are reading.

Be a Sleuth

Look for Clues Does the sequence of the steps matter? What clues help you know the answer?

Ask Questions What questions might a kindergartener ask about making the bookmarks? How would you answer those questions?

Make Your Case Describe what you think is the best way to find your place in a book. Give three reasons why you think that way is best.

Finding a Voice

Caden was unhappy. He had had a difficult surgery. He would be in the hospital for many more weeks. He had a tube in his throat, so he could not talk. How could he tell his mom or dad that he wanted something? How could he talk with friends who came to visit?

One day a nurse had an idea. She found a special tool for him to use. Caden's eyes lit up when she gave it to him. The tool looked like a computer keyboard with a screen. Caden typed a word and then a sentence. When he pushed a button, the computer said whatever Caden had typed! Caden could even choose the voice the computer used and how fast it spoke.

May I please have a glass of water?

It's great to see you today!

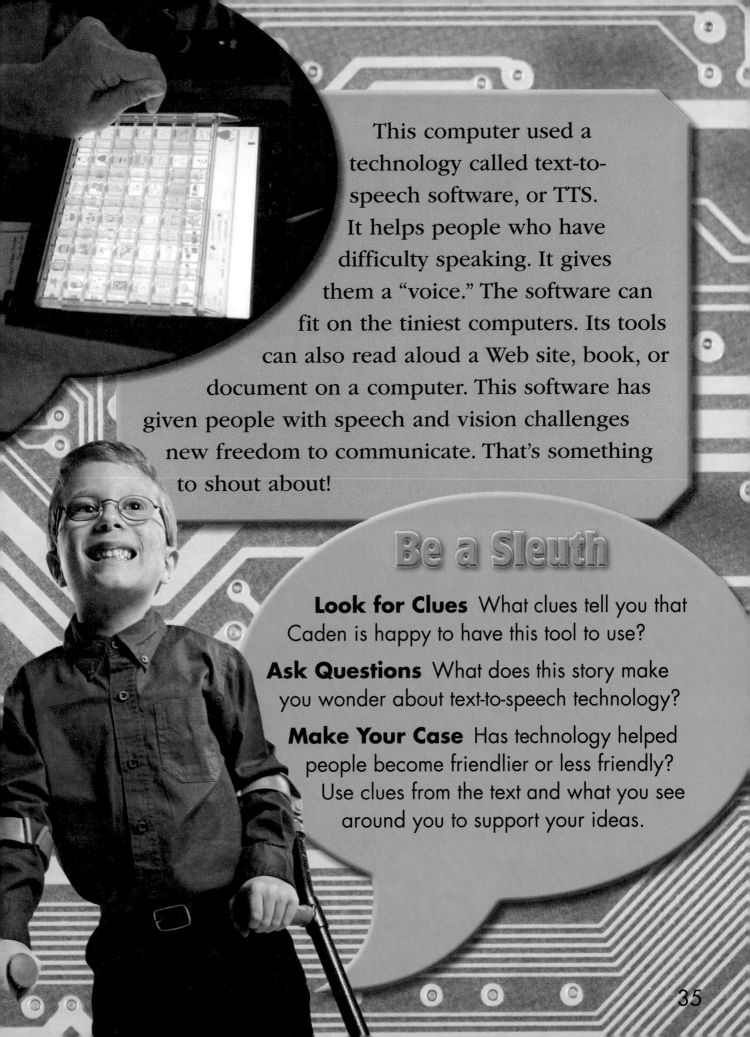

This computer used a technology called text-to-speech software, or TTS. It helps people who have difficulty speaking. It gives them a "voice." The software can fit on the tiniest computers. Its tools can also read aloud a Web site, book, or document on a computer. This software has given people with speech and vision challenges new freedom to communicate. That's something to shout about!

Be a Sleuth

Look for Clues What clues tell you that Caden is happy to have this tool to use?

Ask Questions What does this story make you wonder about text-to-speech technology?

Make Your Case Has technology helped people become friendlier or less friendly? Use clues from the text and what you see around you to support your ideas.

A Birthday Surprise

"Mom will be so surprised!" Sadie said. She looked proudly at the cake that Uncle Curt had helped her and her brother Sam make for Mom's birthday.

"Let's put it in the dining room," Sam said. "That way it will be the first thing Mom sees."

Sadie agreed, and Sam carefully picked it up. Then trouble arrived. Their cousin Wes bounded through the swinging door. The door bumped the plate, the plate tipped, and *splat!* The cake landed on the floor.

"Oh, no!" Sadie cried. "What can we do now?"

"We'll have to be creative," Sam said.

Uncle Curt had made them pancakes that morning before he left for work, and they still had leftovers. "We can't give Mom a birthday cake. Let's give her birthday pancakes instead!" Sadie said.

"Great idea!" said Sam. They warmed the pancakes. Sam spread jam on each one. Then Sadie put on banana slices. They stacked the pancakes and put candles on top.

Just then, they heard Mom coming down the stairs. Sam raced to the stairs and asked her to stay in her bedroom. Mom thought there might be a surprise. Then Sadie arrived with the birthday pancakes. Mom laughed. "How did you know that I have always wanted to have a birthday breakfast in bed?" she said.

Be a Sleuth

Look for Clues What clues tell you about Sadie's talents and personality?

Ask Questions What questions would you have asked if you had been there when the cake fell?

Make Your Case Is it more fun to give a gift or get a gift? Support you answer with your own ideas and ideas from the story.

An Unexpected Gift

Trevor was surprised to get a package from his grandpa. His birthday was still months away.

"Open it," his dad said.

Trevor ripped off the paper, and a note slipped to the floor. He picked it up and read it aloud.

"Dear Trevor, I thought you might like a new challenge."

Trevor opened the box and discovered three balls.

"What am I supposed to do with these?" Trevor asked.

"You juggle them," Dad said.

Trevor tried juggling, but the balls bounced everywhere. He packed the balls away and quickly forgot about them.

The next week Trevor's teacher announced a talent show. There would be prizes for the best acts. Trevor was eager to win a prize, but how? He remembered the balls from his grandpa. But Trevor didn't know how to juggle. What could he do? There was only a month before the show.

Trevor found a book about learning how to juggle and practiced every afternoon. Soon he could juggle the balls.

Trevor invited his grandpa to the show. Trevor's practice paid off. He won first prize! But the best prize of all was seeing his grandpa in the front row, grinning from ear to ear.

Be a Sleuth

Look for Clues What clues show you how Trevor felt about the gift at first?

Make Your Case Do you think talent or practice is more important to being successful at learning how to do something new? Give three reasons to support your answer.

Ask Questions Find a person who had a different answer to the question about whether talent or practice is more important. Ask that person a question about his or her opinion.

A Sweet Treat, Plus a Whole Lot More

Do you like strawberries? When you think of strawberries, maybe you think of a nice breakfast. Maybe to you strawberries are a yummy dessert. However, in many Native American cultures strawberries are much more than food.

Native Americans used the berries to make red dye. It was beautiful and long lasting. They colored cloth, animal skins, and even parts of their own bodies with it.

Native Americans also made medicine from strawberry plants. Some turned the leaves into a tea. The tea helped people who had stomach and kidney problems. Native Americans also made pastes out of the leaves and deer fat. These pastes healed burns and sores.

Crushed berries could even be used to clean teeth! Some Native Americans even used strawberry plants to smell better. They made pads out of the leaves.

They put the pads inside their clothes to smell fresh.

Of course, Native Americans ate the strawberries too. They ate them fresh. They made jams or dried them. Then they could enjoy strawberries all year.

Some Native American groups held a Strawberry Thanksgiving every June. They danced and sang—and ate lots of strawberries! They wanted to show how much they enjoyed this special fruit.

Be a Sleuth

Look for Clues Which uses for strawberry plants would you group together? Why?

Ask Questions What is one question you have about how Native Americans used things in their environment? Where could you look to find an answer to your question?

Make Your Case Find out about another plant that has many uses. Compare this to the uses of the strawberry plant. Which plant is more useful to people? Use reasons to support your choice.

Unit 4
Our Changing World

Hi, Sleuthhounds!
In this unit, you will be looking for clues about how things change. Here are some sleuth tips to help you. You're on the right track!

Sleuth Tips

Look for Clues

How do sleuths remember clues?

- Sleuths don't expect to remember everything. They write down important details.
- Sleuths use many ways to remember clues. They might write a list or draw a picture.

Ask Questions

Why do sleuths ask questions?

- Sleuths ask questions to gather facts. These are often the easiest questions to answer.
- Sleuths also ask questions to make everyone think.

Make Your Case

How do sleuths work with other sleuths?

- Sleuths ask other people questions to find areas where everyone agrees.
- Sleuths want to hear ideas from others.

Prove It!

What do sleuths think about before showing what they have learned?

- Sleuths review what they have learned to decide what's important and what's not.
- Sleuths think about the best order to put things in before sharing them.

The Blank Book

Elias's dad was in the army. He was leaving home to be stationed in another country. As he said good-bye, Dad gave Elias a book. "I want you to read this when you get home," Dad said.

Elias didn't feel like reading, but he opened the book anyway . . . and what a surprise! Every page was blank except the first one. There, Dad explained that they would take turns writing in the book, mailing it back and forth while Dad was gone.

Elias began writing immediately, telling his dad how much he missed him, and then he mailed the book. Three weeks later, the book came back. Dad wrote about a market he had visited. He described the sharp, spicy smells and bright, patterned carpets. He described the warm, buttery bread he tried.

Elias and his dad wrote often. Dad described what life was like on the base. Sometimes he invented silly stories or drew neat pictures. Elias wrote about home and school. He drew colorful pictures. They had to get another book before long, and then another!

When Dad came home, he had a new book with him. "I thought we could keep going," Dad said, grinning. Elias nodded. This was definitely a tradition he wanted to keep.

Be a Sleuth

Look for Clues Find clues that show how what Dad wrote in the book was similar to and different from what Elias wrote.

Ask Questions If you were Elias, what questions might you want to ask Dad about where he was living?

Make Your Case What is the best way to communicate with family members or friends who are far away? Provide reasons to support your answer.

From Seed to Flower to Fruit

Do you know where apples come from? Have you ever seen an apple seed? Inside that tiny brown shell is the beginning of a whole new tree!

Every seed contains an embryo, or a baby plant. The seed protects the baby plant. Then when the seed gets the right amount of water and warmth, it breaks open. The embryo begins to grow.

A stem with little seed leaves pushes upward. There may be one leaf or two leaves. The seedling wants light to help it grow. Roots also begin to grow. They help the seedling get food from the soil.

New leaves grow from the stem. When there are enough new leaves, the seed leaves fall off. Soon flower buds appear. When the flowers open, bees move pollen from one flower

to another. New seeds form inside the flowers. The part of the plant where these seeds are grows larger. It becomes a tiny apple, and soon it will be ready to eat. Do you see the seeds inside? Each seed is ready for a chance to become a new plant. The cycle begins again!

Be a Sleuth

Look for Clues Use clues from the text to draw a picture of how an apple grows from a seed. Add labels to your picture.

Ask Questions What questions would you ask a gardener if you planned on growing your own apple tree?

Make Your Case Should all food plants be grown naturally without using bug spray or plant food? Give reasons for your opinion.

Digging Deep

Do you think there is a lot of activity on Earth's surface? You should see what is going on below us! What happens deep in the Earth can have a big effect on what happens where we live.

The layer we walk and live on is called the crust. It is Earth's thinnest layer. The thickest part is about 25 miles (40 km) deep. The thinnest part is about 3 miles (5 km) deep. That is at the bottom of the ocean.

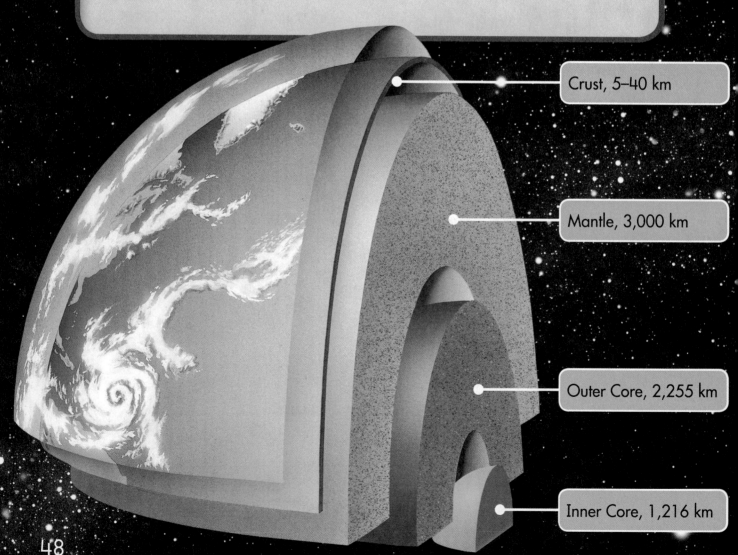

Crust, 5–40 km

Mantle, 3,000 km

Outer Core, 2,255 km

Inner Core, 1,216 km

Below the crust is a layer called the mantle. It is the thickest layer—almost 1,864 miles (3,000 km) thick. It is much hotter than the crust. In fact, it is so hot that rocks can melt! Sometimes, the melted rock can flow out onto the crust as lava. That's how volcanoes form.

Under the mantle, in Earth's center is a super-hot core. The outer part of the core is liquid. The inner part is solid. Scientists think that heat rising up from the core may be one cause of earthquakes. They also think the inner core spins in place. It creates an invisible magnetic shield that protects us from the sun. Scientists keep digging to learn how these lower layers affect our world.

Be a Sleuth

Look for Clues Write two clues you find in the text about how Earth's lower layers affect activity on the crust.

Ask Questions What are two interesting questions you might ask a scientist who studies Earth's layers, volcanoes, or earthquakes?

Make Your Case What layer of Earth would be most interesting to study? Explain your choice. Help others understand why you think it is the most interesting.

The Best Year Ever

"I won't go!" said Aliya. "I won't!" Her mother looked at her, a little frustrated. All weekend, Aliya declared she would not go to second grade. Now, Aliya sat on her bed and refused to get dressed.

"I don't want to go," Aliya said, with tears in her eyes. "Ms. Tresnor made first grade the best year ever. She had a frog *and* a lizard in the classroom. How can second be better?"

"How do you know that it can't?" Mom asked. "Maybe it will be more fun than first grade."

Aliya stood up and slowly pulled on her clothes. After breakfast,

Mom walked her to the bus stop. Soon she was standing outside the door of Mr. Lee's second-grade class. When the door opened, she heard music playing. Then she peeked inside. The classroom was cheerful, and Mr. Lee looked friendly. Aliya saw funny posters on the walls. She spotted a terrarium with a turtle—her favorite animal. And, best of all, she saw her friends Kendra and Jackson. By the time class started, Aliya was sure second grade was going to be the best year ever!

Be a Sleuth

Look for Clues What change was Aliya afraid of, and why was she scared? What clues in the story help you answer these questions?

Ask Questions What questions did you have about second grade before the year started?

Make Your Case What would you say to convince a first grader that second grade could be a great experience? Give at least three reasons.

Too Much of a Good Thing

The farmer sat in his truck and watched the rain fall. The fields were soaked. The water was standing in puddles and ditches. More rain was on its way. The farmer had good reason to worry.

Water is very important. Without water, seeds can't sprout. Plants can't get nutrients from the soil. Leaves can't make food. However, too much water can be a major problem. Heavy rains and flooding can slow growth, damage fruit, wash away soil, and kill plants.

When there is a lot of rain or a flood, the ground soaks up water. Water quickly fills all the spaces in the soil. The plant roots cannot easily get oxygen, so the plants starve. Fruits and vegetables often get bacteria that make them unsafe to eat. They can rot quickly because of all the moisture.

Researchers have found ways to save plants in many flooded areas. There are ways to safely wash away bacteria from some food crops. There are new ways to repair fields and give crops an oxygen boost. Too much water is still a problem for farmers, but it no longer always means a lost crop. That is good news when wet weather strikes.

Be a Sleuth

Look for Clues What are some effects of too much water on plants?

Ask Questions Write one question you have about how weather helps and hurts plants.

Make Your Case Does weather help the farmer more than it hurts him? Explain your opinion using clues from the text.

Unit 5
Responsibility

Hello, Sleuthhounds!
In this unit, you will be looking for clues about responsibility. Here are some sleuth tips to help you. Keep it up!

Sleuth Tips

Look for Clues

How do sleuths uncover clues from an author?

- Sleuths look for clues about sequence or how one event caused another.
- Sleuths work while they read. They try to make the clues fit together like a puzzle.

Ask Questions

Where do sleuths get answers to their questions?

- Sleuths find some answers in the words and pictures. They also talk to other sleuths.
- Sleuths look for answers in other books or on computers.

Make Your Case

How do sleuths use clues when they make a case?

- Sleuths tell what they think. They tell how the clues led them to an answer.
- Sleuths tell where they found the clues. This can be very useful.

Prove It!

Why do sleuths think about who will read what they write?

- Sleuths know that one type of writing doesn't work for every reader.
- Sleuths write in the form that is needed. Sometimes a sleuth writes a list. Sometimes a story or poem is what is needed.

Firehouse Friends

If you visit a fire station, you might be greeted with a wagging tail and a wet kiss. Dalmatians have been firefighting mascots for years. Many fire stations are homes for these black-and-white dogs. But how did they become a firefighter's best friend?

Dalmatians are friendly, smart, and strong. They also seem to get along well with horses. In the days before cars and trucks, firefighters used to use horse-drawn carriages. People taught Dalmatians to be "coach dogs." Dalmatians ran alongside coaches pulled by horses. They protected the horses and people from stray dogs and other animals. They kept the horses calm. Horse theft was a common problem too. Dalmatians stayed with the horses when the carriage stopped to guard them from thieves.

Even though horses are no longer used by firefighters, Dalmatians still live in some fire stations today. Firefighters spend long hours at the firehouse. They have to be ready for the alarm to sound. Days or even weeks can go by without a fire to put out. Dalmatians make good companions for firefighters.

Be a Sleuth

Look for Clues What clues in the text explain how Dalmatians first became connected to firefighters? What clues explain why Dalmatians can still be found in some fire stations?

Ask Questions Write two interesting questions you still have about Dalmatians.

Make Your Case Caring for animals can be expensive. Should communities pay for firefighters to keep pets? Provide reasons to support your opinion.

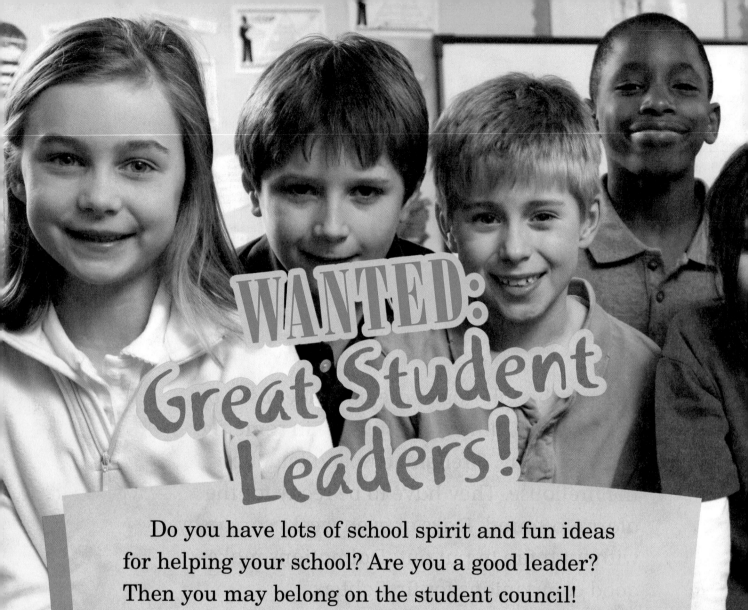

WANTED: Great Student Leaders!

Do you have lots of school spirit and fun ideas for helping your school? Are you a good leader? Then you may belong on the student council!

Many schools have student councils. These are groups of students who are chosen to share ideas and make decisions about student activities. Students often elect student council members in a class or grade-level election. Council members work hard to be good students, good citizens, and good examples to everyone at school.

Some students are officers with special duties. They lead the council meetings, keep records, and work with school staff members. Others are representatives. They talk to the students in their classes to get ideas. Later, they report

58

back to the class about decisions the student council has made.

But what does a student council actually *do?* It might organize an event, such as a school carnival. It might raise money for new equipment. It might plan volunteer activities, such as a food drive, to help people in the community. If there is a problem in the school, the student council may discuss possible solutions to the problem.

Are you ready to make a difference in your school? If so, the student council may be the place for you!

Be a Sleuth

Look for Clues What are some clues that you find in the pictures and text that help you better understand what a student council does?

Ask Questions What questions might you have for students on a student council?

Make Your Case What do you think is the most important trait a student should have to be on a student council? Give reasons to explain your thinking.

DONATION BOX

Stretch, My Pet Giraffe

"You won't believe what I found!" I said.

"What is it, dear?" Mom asked, looking at me.

"A giraffe!" I cried. "Can I keep it?"

"I'm not sure how it would fit in our house," Mom said.

I answered, "Oh, this is just a baby. She can sleep in my room."

"Well, I guess we can try it," Mom said.

I went to get my new pet, Stretch, but she was taller than I remembered. That wasn't the only problem. No sooner had she followed me into the living room than she saw Mom's lemon tree. Stretch began eating the leaves. Mom didn't look too happy.

I checked on the computer to see what to feed a giraffe. I found out giraffes eat as much as sixty pounds of leaves a day! Then I led Stretch down the hall to my room where she quickly began chewing one of my socks. I knew then that my room and my house were clearly not the best home for her.

Now Stretch lives at the zoo, where she has room to grow, friends to play with, and all the leaves she wants to eat. Even better is that my mom's tree is safe, and my socks don't have holes in them!

Be a Sleuth

Look for Clues What clues let you know that Stretch was not a good choice for a pet?

Ask Questions What are three questions you have about giraffes and their needs?

Make Your Case Should people be able to keep wild animals as pets? Give reasons to support your opinion.

Unlikely Friends

Every Monday afternoon, Anya helped Ms. Hickson with her yardwork. Ms. Hickson always watched Anya from her tall porch. She even had a glass of juice waiting for her when the work was done. Anya often brought along her violin. Ms. Hickson would beam with delight when Anya played for her. Anya used to complain about visiting Ms. Hickson, but Anya's mother always insisted she go. She said that neighbors should take care of each other.

One Monday, Anya came without her violin. When she finished raking the yard, she sat down sadly beside her neighbor. Ms. Hickson asked what had happened. Anya burst into tears. Her brother had broken her violin by accident. There was no way it could be fixed in time for her fall concert. Ms. Hickson disappeared into the house. She returned a few minutes later with an old violin case. Inside was the most beautiful violin Anya had ever

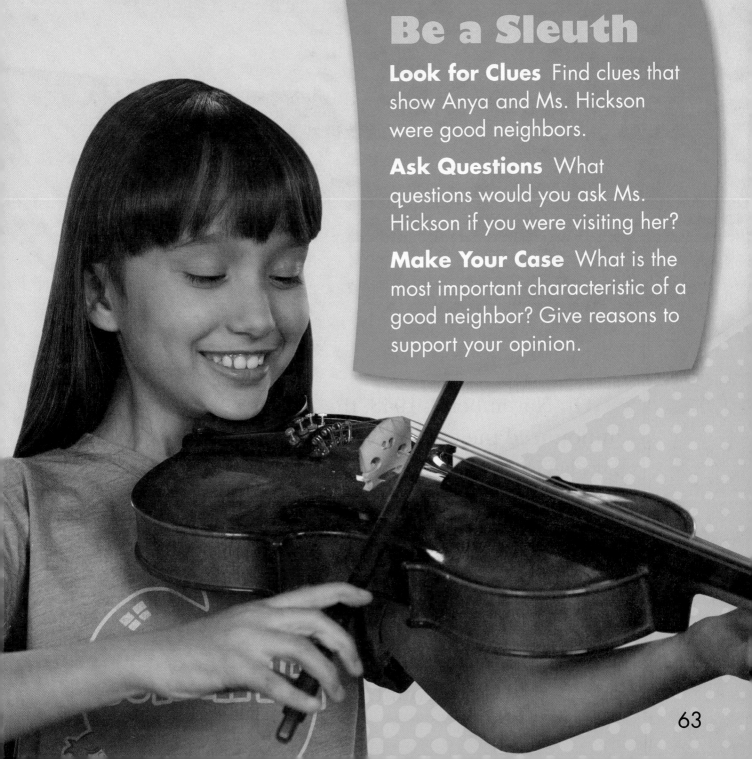

seen. Ms. Hickson picked it up lovingly and handed it to Anya. Anya played a few notes, laid the violin in its velvet-lined case, and threw her arms around Ms. Hickson. The violin was the best gift Anya had ever received.

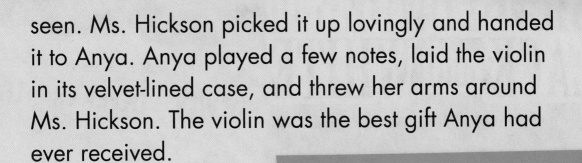

Be a Sleuth

Look for Clues Find clues that show Anya and Ms. Hickson were good neighbors.

Ask Questions What questions would you ask Ms. Hickson if you were visiting her?

Make Your Case What is the most important characteristic of a good neighbor? Give reasons to support your opinion.

A BIG BLUNDER in BLACK and WHITE

Chicago Daily Tribune
Home

DEWEY DEFEATS TRUMAN

On November 3, 1948, the newspaper headline announced the winner of the election: "DEWEY DEFEATS TRUMAN." Harry Truman was the President of the United States. Thomas Dewey was running for President against him. That headline became the most famous headline in history because it was wrong. In fact, Truman actually won the election.

The *Chicago Daily Tribune* was one of the biggest newspapers in the country. In the days before computers, it took hours to set up a newspaper for printing. The employees at the *Tribune* didn't wait for the final vote count. Because the election was so close, it was difficult to predict who might win. When the news came that Dewey hadn't won after all, the workers were embarrassed. The newspaper had already delivered 150,000 copies with the wrong news!

The newspaper staff scrambled to fix the mistake. They printed the newspaper again with the correct news. The *Tribune* sent out many people to collect the newspapers that were incorrect. By then, however, many people had already seen the mistake.

Even today, people remember that famous mistake. It is a reminder to check the facts and get the news right . . . the first time!

BE A SLEUTH

TRUMAN

Look for Clues Find clues that tell what the staff of the *Tribune* did to try to fix their mistake.

Ask Questions What are some questions that you would ask if you were a newspaper reporter writing about an election?

Make Your Case What do you think is the right thing to do if a newspaper or television program makes a mistake in a news story?

Unit 6
Traditions

Calling all Sleuthhounds!

In this unit, you will be looking for clues about traditions and celebrations. Here are some sleuth tips to help you. Here we go!

Sleuth Tips

Look for Clues

How do sleuths know if a clue is important?

- Sleuths find and record many clues. They don't always know which clues will be the important ones.
- Sleuths look for ways to fit the clues together.

Ask Questions

How do sleuths think of interesting questions to ask?

- Sleuths often ask for more information about a clue.
- Sleuths think about the questions that have not been answered.

Make Your Case

How do sleuths learn from other sleuths?

- Sleuths listen to others. What clues did they find?
- Sleuths ask questions to understand what others are thinking.

Prove It!

How do sleuths prepare to share what they know?

- Sleuths know that most things aren't perfect on the first try. They reread and rewrite to make it better.
- Sleuths get better with practice. Practice makes sharing easier and more fun.

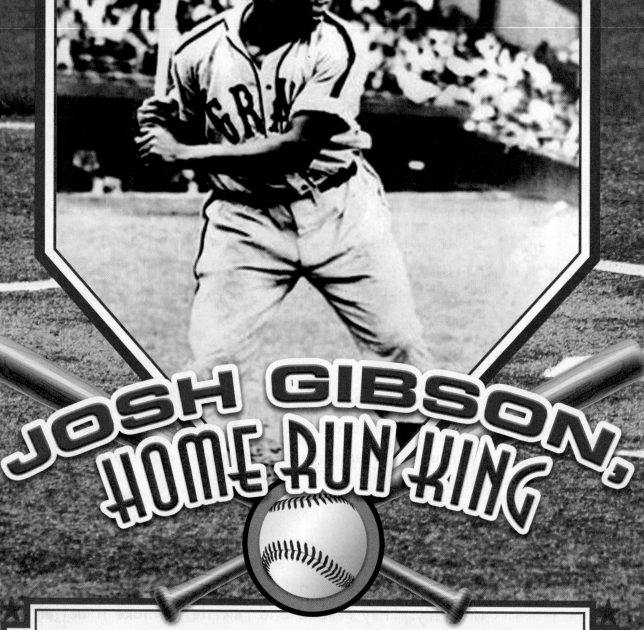

JOSH GIBSON, HOME RUN KING

Josh Gibson's first love was baseball. In his spare time, Gibson could be found improving his skills and showing off his talent. One night in 1930, Gibson went to watch his hometown team, the Homestead Grays, play against the Kansas City Monarchs. That night changed everything.

The Grays' catcher was injured. The team's owner remembered seeing eighteen-year-old Gibson play ball. He invited the young athlete to play that night. The owner was so impressed that he asked Gibson to join the team. Gibson played professional baseball for the rest of his life.

Josh Gibson was a great player. He hit hundreds of home runs. Gibson led the Negro National League in home runs for ten years. He could hit a baseball harder and farther than almost any other player in the history of the game. He was a skilled catcher too. He earned a place in the Baseball Hall of Fame. But Josh Gibson didn't play in the Major Leagues. The Major Leagues were closed to African American players at the time. Three months after Gibson's death in 1947, Jackie Robinson became the first African American to play in the Major Leagues. He carried on Gibson's tradition of baseball excellence.

BE A SLEUTH

Look for Clues What clues can you find that show baseball was important to Josh Gibson?

Ask Questions What are three interesting questions you wonder about that are related to baseball long ago?

Make Your Case The United States has a long tradition of enjoying sports. What do you think is America's favorite sport? Give three reasons for your opinion.

Respecting the Star-Spangled Banner

You've probably seen hundreds of American flags in all different sizes. They can be found at schools and government buildings. They decorate parks and bridges. They are carried in parades. The American flag is recognized around the world as a symbol of the United States. The Federal Flag Code tells how the flag should be displayed. It states, "No disrespect should be shown to the flag of the United States of America."

The flag is even folded in a special way to show respect. Give it a try!

First, hold the end of the flag that has stars. Hold it at both corners while a friend holds the other two corners. Fold the flag in half lengthwise. The long striped section will be on top. Then fold it in half lengthwise again. The stars should be showing again at your end.

Next, while you hold your end, your friend should fold one corner to the opposite edge to make a triangle. He or she repeats these triangle folds until only the stars are showing. Tuck in the last triangle to finish folding the flag. Now you can put the folded flag away safely, knowing that you have respected an important symbol for our country.

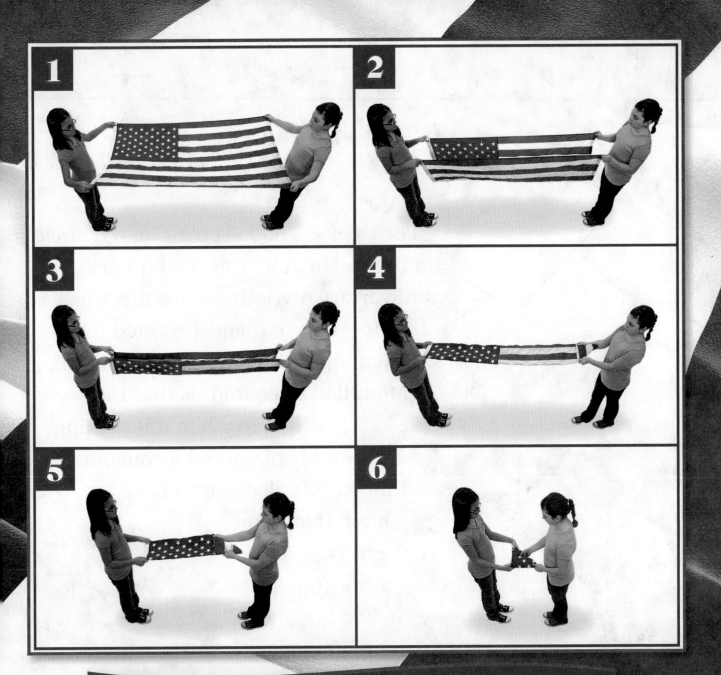

Be a Sleuth

Look for Clues Why does the order of the instructions for folding the flag matter?

Ask Questions What questions do you have about caring for or displaying the American flag?

Make Your Case How would you convince someone that it is important to show respect for the flag? Give at least three reasons why it matters.

Another Movie Night to Remember

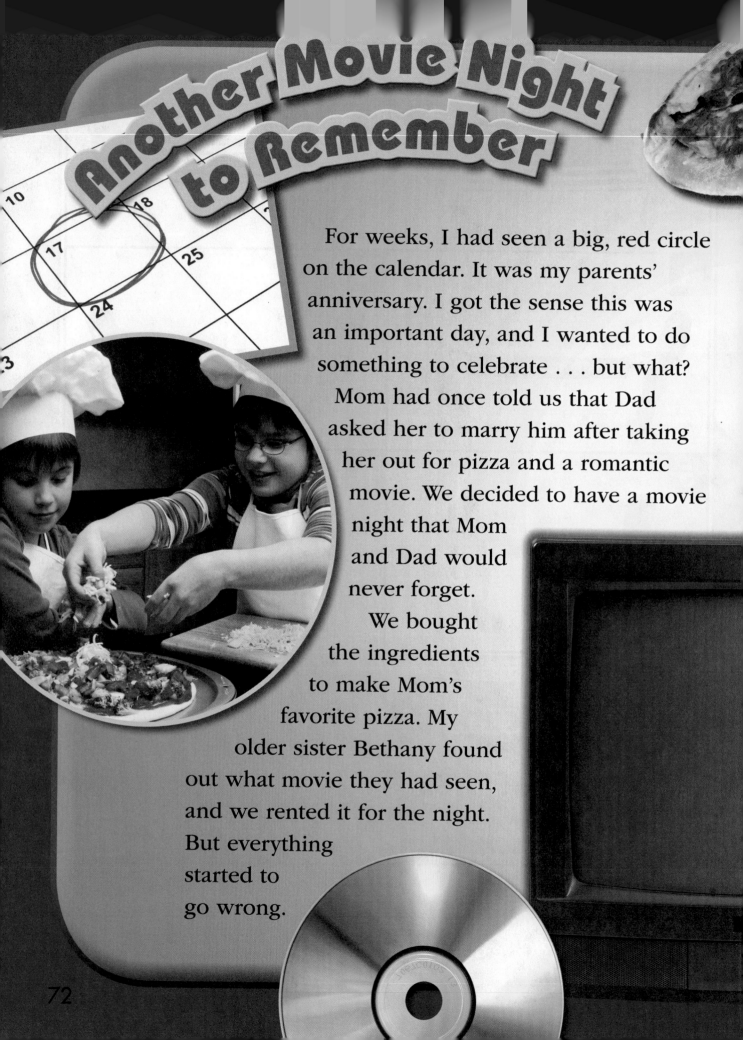

For weeks, I had seen a big, red circle on the calendar. It was my parents' anniversary. I got the sense this was an important day, and I wanted to do something to celebrate . . . but what? Mom had once told us that Dad asked her to marry him after taking her out for pizza and a romantic movie. We decided to have a movie night that Mom and Dad would never forget.

We bought the ingredients to make Mom's favorite pizza. My older sister Bethany found out what movie they had seen, and we rented it for the night. But everything started to go wrong.

First, the pizza slid off the pan and onto the floor as I carried it to the table. Next, Bethany burned the popcorn, so the whole house smelled awful. Then we discovered that the DVD wouldn't play. Bethany and I were upset, but Dad chuckled as he opened a window to air out the house. He took us out to dinner, to the same restaurant where he and Mom had eaten that special night. Over pizza, we heard the story of how Mom and Dad met. It was better than the best romantic movie—even without popcorn!

Be a Sleuth

Look for Clues What clues can you find to show that Mom and Dad were not upset about the problems that happened with the surprise?

Ask Questions What questions would you ask someone who is celebrating a special day?

Make Your Case What celebration or tradition is most important to you? Give at least two reasons why it is special.

CURTIS THE COWBOY COOK

Curtis was bored and unhappy. He thought when he was hired to work on the cattle drive that he'd finally get to be a real cowboy. But the cowboys treated him like a kid. The cook, Dusty, let Curtis help him. But Dusty was so busy he barely had time to talk. Curtis just watched and did chores for the cook all day long.

The chuckwagon always went ahead of the slow-moving cattle. That way, dinner would be ready when the cowboys got to camp each night. Dusty and Curtis started the cooking fire. As they carried water from a creek, Dusty slipped down the bank. He landed hard. Curtis helped Dusty limp painfully to camp. Then Curtis got to work with Dusty directing him.

He cut the salt pork and arranged it in deep pans. He scooped beans into the pans, covered them with water, and set them on the fire to boil. Soon the contents of the pans were bubbling, and the smell filled the camp. As the sun went down, the tired, hungry cowboys arrived. One bite of the hearty pork and beans was enough to convince them that Curtis was born to be a cowboy cook.

BE A SLEUTH

Look for Clues What clues can you find that show how the cowboys' feelings about Curtis change from the beginning to the end of the story?

Ask Questions What are two questions you have about cowboys and cattle drives?

Make Your Case Being a cowboy seemed like an exciting way of life to Curtis. What kind of work might someone like Curtis think would be exciting today? Give reasons for your ideas.

THE UNION MUST AND SHALL BE PRESERVED

FREE SPEECH.
FREE HOMES.
FREE TERRITORY.

PROTECTION TO AMERICAN INDUSTRY

FOR PRESIDENT
ABRAHAM LINCOLN
OF ILLINOIS

FOR VICE PRESIDENT
HANNIBAL HAMLIN
OF MAINE

KENNEDY JOHNSON

What does it take to become President of the United States? A good candidate would be a leader. A good candidate would be a strong, honest person and a hard worker. A good candidate would have plans for leading the country. How do candidates get people's attention? They talk to people, advertise, and take part in debates. Many also use clever slogans. Candidates have been using slogans for a very long time.

Some slogans remind people of history. William Henry Harrison was a hero at the Battle of Tippecanoe in 1811. In 1840, he wanted to be President and wanted John Tyler as the Vice

President. He used the slogan "Tippecanoe and Tyler too!" to remind voters that he was a military hero.

Some slogans make promises. In 1928, Herbert Hoover used the slogan "A chicken in every pot and a car in every garage." Hoover wanted voters to think of the good things they could have if the economy improved.

Other slogans try to make people feel good. Dwight Eisenhower was nicknamed Ike, and he used "I like Ike" as his campaign slogan for the 1952 election.

Look at the slogans in the pictures. What do you think these candidates wanted voters to believe?

Be a Sleuth

Look for Clues What are the purposes of campaign slogans, according to the text?

Ask Questions What are two questions you would ask someone who wanted to be President of the United States?

Make Your Case Should there be rules for the kinds of slogans candidates use? Give reasons to support your ideas.

Acknowledgments

Photographs

Every effort has been made to secure permission and provide appropriate credit for photographic material. The publisher deeply regrets any omission and pledges to correct errors called to its attention in subsequent editions.

Unless otherwise acknowledged, all photographs are the property of Pearson Education, Inc.

Photo locators denoted as follows: Top (T), Center (C), Bottom (B), Left (L), Right (R), Background (Bkgd)

Cover

Chandler Digital Art

4 (TL) ©kontur-vid/Fotolia, (Bkgrd) ©Nightman1965/Fotolia, (C) ©Warakorn/Fotolia, (TR) ©Zedcor Wholly Owned/Thinkstock, (C) Shutterstock; **5** (CR) ©PaulPaladin/Fotolia, (BR) Fotolia, (TR) Hemera Technologies/Thinkstock; **8** (C) Kim Karpeles /Alamy Images; **10** (Bkgrd) NASA; **12** (Bkgrd) ©Royal Geographical Society/Alamy Images; **14** (C) ©Derrick Neill/Fotolia, (Bkgrd) ©Natalia Pavlova/Fotolia; **16** (C) Mary Evans Picture Library/Alamy Images, (Bkgrd) Tom Brakefield/Thinkstock; **17** (TR) ©tanya18/Fotolia, (B) Photos/Thinkstock; **20** (Bkgrd) ©Kit Wai Chan/Fotolia; **21** (C) Stockbyte/Thinkstock; **22** (B) ©David M Schrader/Fotolia, (BC) ©iMagine/Fotolia, (T) ©lacabetyar/Fotolia, (C) ©mates/Fotolia, (C) Thinkstock; **24** (T) Care Bags Foundation; **26** (C) ©photka/Fotolia, (T) ©picsfive/Fotolia, (Bkgrd) Melinda Fawver/Shutterstock; **27** (C) ©Stockbyte/Thinkstock; **28** (T) ©Elnur/Fotolia, (C) ©Jupiterimages/Thinkstock, (BL) Shane Trotter/Shutterstock; **29** (BR) ©uwimages/Fotolia; **32** (C) ©Alexey Belikov/Fotolia, (C) ©Alexey Novikov/Fotolia, (Bkgrd) ©annavee/Fotolia; **34** (Bkgrd) ©pzAxe/Fotolia; **35** (T) ©ZUMA Press/NewsCom, (BL) Thinkstock; **36** (B) ©Elenathewise/Fotolia; **38** (B) ©Getty Images/Thinkstock, (T) ©hfng/Fotolia, (Bkgrd) ©Mahesh Patil/Fotolia, (C) ©Silkstock/Fotolia, (TL) ©Svetlana Gryankina/Fotolia; **40** (C) ©araos/Fotolia, (BR) ©Monkey Business/Fotolia, (Bkgrd) Alina G/Shutterstock; **41** (TR) ©Harris Shiffman/Fotolia, (TR) ©Ivan Josifovic/Fotolia; **44** (T) ©Barbara Helgason/Fotolia, (B) ©Douglas Freer/Fotolia, (BL) ©gaelj/Fotolia, (Bkgrd) ©javarman/Fotolia; **45** (BR) ©Victor B/Fotolia, (TR) Thinkstock; **46** (T) ©Dynamic Graphics/Thinkstock, (BR) ©Jenny Thompson/Fotolia, (Bkgrd) ©Justimagine/Fotolia, (C) Geoff Dann/©DK Images, (TL) James Stevenson/©DK Images; **47** (TL) ©unpict/Fotolia, (BR) Hemera Technologies/Thinkstock; **48** (B) ©DK Images, (Bkgrd) Tjefferson/Fotolia; **49** (R) ©Catmando/Fotolia; **50** (Bkgrd) ©Alex_Mac/Fotolia, (B) ©Antalia/Fotolia, (C) ©picsfive/Fotolia, (BL) Bananastock/Thinkstock; **51** (BR) ©Fotomag/Fotolia; **52** (TL) ©dusk/Fotolia, (BL) ©Harvey Hudson/Fotolia, (Bkgrd) Paul Orr/Shutterstock; **53** (R) ©Matauw/Fotolia, (TR) ©Sinisa Botas/Fotolia; **56** (B) ©Amy Walters/Fotolia, (C) ©dexns/Fotolia, (T) ©Eric Isselee/Fotolia, (C) ©wakuka/Fotolia; **57** (T) ©LeDo/Fotolia; **58** (T) ©Monkey Business/Fotolia; **59** (B) ©mangostock/Fotolia; **60** (B) ©DigitalGenetics/Fotolia, (TL) ©Franco Deriu/Fotolia; **61** (R) ©Andrey Sukhachev/Fotolia, (R) ©Thorsten Schmitt/Fotolia, (B) Photodisc/Thinkstock; **62** (TL) ©Alexei Norikov/Fotolia; **63** (B) Digital Vision/Thinkstock; **64** (TL) ©Everett Collection Inc/Alamy Images; **65** (B) ©M. Dykstra/Fotolia, (R) ©zentilla/Fotolia; **68** (Bkgrd) ©Jim Mills/Fotolia, (TC) National Baseball Hall of Fame Library, Cooperstown, NY; **70** (Bkgrd) ©SSilver/Fotolia; **72** (CL) ©Glenda Powers/Fotolia, (BR) ©Gudellaphoto/Fotolia, (BC) ©Kredo/Fotolia, (TL) ©Sharpshot/Fotolia; **73** (CL) ©Jupiterimages/Thinkstock, (TC) ©Laurent Renault/Fotolia, (TL) ©sax/Fotolia; **74** (B) ©Kevin Largent/Fotolia, (Bkgrd) Comstock/Thinkstock; **75** (TR) ©Jupiterimages/Fotolia, (BL) ©Sarunya_foto/Fotolia; **76** (Bkgrd) ©vege/Fotolia, (T) Prints & Photographs Division, Library of Congress, (CR) Steve Wood/Shutterstock; **77** (TR) Prints & Photographs Division, Library of Congress.